An Argument for a 4th Branch of U.S. Government

To Outlaw Harmful Deception by our Government and Corporations

by

Michael C. Longo

Balance Books
Lula, Georgia USA

Published by the Three H Company/Balance Books, which is my publishing company with three titles, Shining Like the Sun, The Trinity Balance, and this one.

 ISBN: 978-0-9676704-2-3 by The 3H Company/Balance Books. Library of Congress Control Number: Not listed yet

Dedicated to

We the People aka the good people of the United States

And the Preamble to the U.S. Constitution Goals

Note: This is a work in progress. I hope you chime in and add what you think is overlooked or stands in its way on the Creating Paradise YouTube, Rumble, and X channels. As more data, clarity in this proposal, and events happen concerning this project more content will be added in future renditions. This is rendition 10.

Thoughts from our founders

Follow the truth where ever it may lead
Thomas Jefferson

You will never know how much it has cost my generation to preserve your freedom. I hope you will make a good use of it.
John Adams

The natural process of things is for liberty to yield, and the government to gain ground.
Thomas Jefferson
(It is this very thing we are fighting against as the ground gain of late is fraught with illegalities and moral decay that is repugnant to the constitution of which this nation stands.)

We have no government armed with power capable of contending with human passions unbridled by morality and religion...Our constitution was made only for a moral and religious people. It is wholly inadequate to the government of any other.
John Adams

Law is whatever is boldly asserted and plausibly maintained.
Aaron Burr

Those that can give up essential liberty to gain a little temporary safety deserve neither liberty or safety.
Benjamin Franklin

Table of Contents

Forward

“What country can preserve its liberties if their rulers are not warned from time to time that their people preserve the spirit of resistance?”—Thomas Jefferson

243 years ago, the U.S. Constitution was ratified and added to over time and became the guiding document that We the People created so that a people-representative government could be tasked with forging a path over time to ensure the six benefits stated in the preamble of the U.S. Constitution by the government. One safeguard was put in, the 2nd amendment, to make sure the government did not get out of hand in its mission. But the safeguard has proven to be wholly inadequate as we will soon herein.

On July 4th, 1776 our founders declared us independent from its mother country, England. Today, July 4th 2023 I declare we need a 4th branch of Government to make sure that the information the public and the 3 branches use to decide things is free of harmful deception. With this almost private declaration as it is today, it will become known as a new birthday, the day the declaration to real freedom began. Because when you are bathed in the real truths that matter in your life, you are set free to be all you can be. And when the whole of the nation makes that its priority then the six goals of the preamble can be easily met.

I hope I have made a good argument in the content that follows. Know this is doable, we the people created the government, made the amendments, and now as things stand, we the people cannot add another, we need those in power to decide that. No, I don’t think that is right, do you? We, therefore, have a bit of a trick path to get to the 4th branch empowered to stop deception, but again, it is doable. It is my hope that you will help spread this declaration to end the harmful deception in our country’s leaders and corporations.

One more thing before we begin, I want this proposal to come from We the People so in this very first edition, read it and find what you like and don't like then let me know. I will make the additions and thank you in the acknowledgments for all those that help here. This, therefore, needs a We the People movement, so see if you can add to it, or find flaws that make it less likely to be a reality. For me, I see other choices since the idea of storming the castle with guns as a coup of some kind is just not going to happen, Jan 6th taught us that much right? No, if we are to fix things, we have to use the power of truth to do it, and to get there we need to enforce no more harmful deception as that is the key cause of all the shit show material and the weak link in the power structure. True is undeniable, but when you call a lie a truth, then you know you got troubles and a fix of things is in order.

So, no matter where you enter the picture of what is going on with deception, I hope one of my chapters finds your open door so you can get the whole picture of how We the People can fix a corrupt government that was installed by us, it is ours. Yes, I know that can be contested, and that is why this needs all of us to eventually vote this into being. Popular public opinion will outweigh interpretations of the spirit of the constitution so that its true owners and controllers, we the people can have our voice.

Introduction

Why have I put my life on hold to suggest the proposal? First, in order to create Paradise on Earth, which is my goal as it is for many people if not all people, peace on Earth needs to be established. Ending deception can do that leading to other gifts the truth brings. Here I am in the United States in the hope it will spread to the whole of the world. The second thing we need is to stop the harm deception causes since there is no good reason for it, EVER. Third is because it is the right thing to do, and fourth is all of the above. Paradise can only flourish when those who live there are wise enough to create it, so this will be an educational process for all of us as, we the people, learn how to fix the constitution so the government is designed properly to serve us and all life in general. Added that last part due to the overwhelming interest governments worldwide with the US leading to help life via the climate, so yeah, let's do that, let's see the truth about it since there are outstanding allegations from top scientists on how best humans can interact with the atmosphere, land, and seas.

To accomplish this, I suggest we need to weed out harmful deception that does not align with the natural order of things, we call that the absolute truth to calibrate to. Any policy that moves us away from that by deception is harmful and needs to stop ASAP. Everyone senses something is wrong with the way things are going. You'd really have to hide to not see it at this point, but do read on if that describes you, please, and please ask questions from almost anyone, they know. Direct lying to the people is called by many names, propaganda, social programming, brainwashing, and on and on, and those who buy it because they let others think for them will not lead you to answers. You always have to question claimed results to see if they are true and align with nature and reality as over-and-over testing it shows. This we must do as a nation lest we fail as a nation.

I feel this proposal will work to create a branch of the gov that will oversee the other three making sure it does not fall victim to any kind of deception that may arise or is already in play because it will be run by the people to do one simple task. Enforcement will be conducted by the courts and the space force cadets (my suggestion) which does need a means to build its ranks. The 4th Branch will be that beacon on the hill that the other branches will know they are being watched to be honest to carrying out the tasks to make sure the preamble goals are met.

So why me, why is this bloke doing this? Because of the claims in my book The Trinity Balance. It claims to be able to solve any problem in our 3-dimensional world, such was promised to me when I got it from the universe in "74", so I applied it to what we have now in our USA and the whole of this book is what popped out, as an answer, a means to actually keep our government balanced so it can indeed achieve the objectives contained in the preamble. What the Trinity Book talks about is life occurs at its best, always, between the union of opposites that define the whole subject in question. Using this guide can lead anyone to good answers to problems, so here I am with the best answer it can say about the way our government designed to serve the people has failed in so many areas but can be easily fixed by simply being honest so people can use real truths to make the accurate decisions.

I am submitting this proposal at this time as a neutral observer in the "who is better" political process. So, know that I am doing this because I have seen claims and unproven statements from both sides of the ale and I, like many people are sick of it. We have a less than perfect union and that and other goals are not being met as you will read. When we as a nation return to thc goals in the preamble we will be where we thought we were when we began this nation. We simply have to fix our constitution to make sure only real truth is used in the narratives that debate the issues of the day.

Chapter One

State of the Effectiveness of Our US Constitutional Government in meeting the goals set in the preamble.

We the people set this country up to be run by our peers, our friends, and our neighbors each to abide by the restraints in a newly formed structure outlined in the US Constitution wherein certain conditions were to be met on both sides of the deal which we usually refer to as a contract. That will have to be argued in court. So, let's see how we the people, and the gov are holding up their end of the contract, shall we?

So where are we with the state of the Government fulfilling the Preamble goals, and isn't that what the constitution is all about, to create a safe place from the kind of tyranny the founders ran away from, in these new lands. The question is, has the Government sought to provide a perfect Union? Has it established equal Justice to all of its People? Does it seek to create domestic tranquility? Is it providing for out common defense or do what se see in the last 80 years or so it providing a secret agenda that is offensive? Does it promote the general welfare of its people, us? And having done this so well do you think we can pass on our country for as many generations of people as we want? These are the six goals of the preamble and we will take a look at each in a second. To those who already are well aware of our Government's failures in each of these areas, you might want to skip this section and move right to the solution and how to do it chapters.

A more perfect Union

When those in power gaslight the ones they do not agree with, encourage and support the hating of the other party, conduct suspect elections when the blockchain system can secure them, and when our foreign policy hurts our reputation around the world then we do not have a perfect union. This has been a trend of late highlighted by the fact we cannot protect our borders resulting in millions of people flooding our country and taking needed resources that are not going to those citizens and veterans who have given so much to make this a great nation. What is the purpose of letting so many in, and for that matter, why in Europe too? There is an agenda that is not being shared to the countries being literally, invaded. If we are to form a more perfect union then we need to consider not allowing our government and businesses that sell products to us to deceive us in ways that go against the preamble as in causing harm.

Establish Justice

You will first notice injustice The mere fact that we have to sue the gov for breach of contract/agreement/pledge because they have not fullfilled the pure intent of the preamble by in many cases doing the opposite is the single biggest injustice our nation may ever face, we the people hope it is the last example and things straighten out asap. Justice must be blind and follow just laws. Laws that are repugnant to the Constitution's guidelines and spirit of intent are void and invalid. Site the section that says that, please. Soon you will see how the proposed 4th can fix this as for the gov to drift into such behaviors can be amended as we the people have the right to do so using the popular vote, not constitutional Congress as it is those in the system who have not spoken up, why would be leave it to them to do this. Yes, we need a self-correcting government. But let's not get ahead of ourselves, next up is domestic tranquility.

Insure Domestic Tranquility

Illegal immigration, why, why is this going on? We the People would not only like to know that but we would like to how bringing in so many illegals creates domestic tranquility. More accurately, is it gaslighting to say nothing about it and criminal to let it happen? And in today's world, can we even question what is going on without being harmed in some way? That is not tranquility from the government, that is terrorism, so these allegations of harm need to be investigated to say the least. The new structure of the government with is simple addition will make this sort of thing historic and nonexistent.

Provide for the Common Defense

The allegation here is that the military-industrial complex as a profit-making machine has teamed up with an agenda profile aka a plan to make us a military offensive force. Now I understand that being a responsible country that holds the world's reserve currency also comes with the task of being the world's police force that has turned to using a force of another kind to persuade countries to use The USD in their trade, and if you don't, well, read the accounts from one tasked to do the persuading in Confessions of an Economic Hitman. This allegation is made by ... ... who wrote confessions of an economic hitman and has to be taken seriously since what he claims did happen, you only bring us the back story, the evidence of the deceptive tactics to force compliance by those that try to go their own way. And now this heavy-handed enforcement has caused the BRICK nations to grow and actually stop using the USD which threatens our status as the world's reserve currency. That and an out-of-control US Gov US-generated debit, Gov shutdowns, and the rating of our country in Standard and Poors going lower does not add to our overall health as a nation at all, it only makes one worry as to what the gov is actually doing to full fill the preamble goals.

General Welfare

The speech Steve Kirsch gave to Congress easily points out how the GOV and Biz has failed us. He simply asks for the data comparison to be made where he asks the common-sense question, "What is the difference in health states between the unvaxed people and those who got the prescribed multiple shots from day one of life to say 20 years old. From the numbers he could find that are available he found that the unvaxed got 90% fewer health issues than those who got the whole panel of shots recommended by the CDC. The reason he was testifying before Congress is because he could not get large sample size data results from any states or the CDC and no one could tell him who gave the order to not give him the data, clear deception on so many levels affecting the whole of our countries people. Why are his queries being ignored and why is asking such important questions a career-ending path to follow? Who is giving these orders because it is clearly a criminal act to outcast anyone for asking questions. That right there is the basis of our science, the bases of our civilization, is it not? Then why are we the people putting up with it? Why? Because before now, before this proposal we did not have a means in view to stop it due to its vast scope of infection.

Secure the Blessings of Liberty to ourselves and our Posterity.

This goal is put in place that we are to build a nation that will last forever. This is very open to debate right now as the allegations run wild as to the level of harm being done to our country from all sectors right now. With paid-for science blocking real truth the policies of the nation are more aimed at profit than the goals of the constitution at the expense of human lives, human and animal health, to name only two areas that are cause for alarm ....

Seems to me there has been a good deal of deception by those in power to get us to this point, nothing else explains how far from our goals we are at the moment.

Chapter Two

An Argument for Breach of Contract

As we learned in Chapter One, our "created and put in place government", has allegedly gone astray from its mission statement as noted in the preamble. From forever poisons in our lands and water supplies to conducting aggressive, not defensive wars worldwide, our government leaders and policies need to be brought back to their original mission oath. We can do this, restore our nation to the degree where we once again be the light to the world and lead us into being a "class one" galactic civilization, which is noted by those planets who have given up on war as a means to settle disputes. Everything is a learning experience when done in love and not selfishness so why would there be any fighting to the death on any issue?

Before we get into how to sue the gov for breach of contract I want to give you my idea of what we are. We are a soul that exists in another dimension that has expression in this dimension, the 3D world it is sometimes called. In pure form, our soul looks like the sun in the sky as it generates the energy within which gives life to our body. I like to think of it as a nuclear power type system that uses the energy from the cells of the body to be 100s of times stronger that it was in said other dimension.

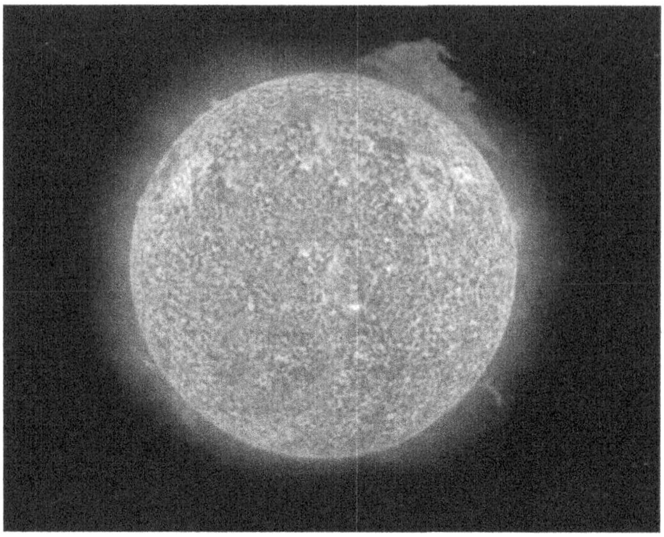

This is us in our purest form. Many have seen orbs and recorded them. They are translucent floating balls of energy. This is a soul traveling without its physical body from where it still needs research to be accurate. Just know that this is how we look in reality, a self-generating ball of energy, and when it interacts with anything, we, are learning, being, and living as a soul, in the physical reality everyone is so focused on, except physicists, naturalists, and spiritual people. The point is the body is the temple to house the soul so that it can learn and grow into what IT, YOU, want due to your life experiences. You will be guided to develop as your soul vibration needs not what anyone else wants.

When this is interrupted by coercion to murder then that right there needs to be stopped, as in full-stop, and usually is on an individual level (unless you are a targeted individual). Only now, on a global scale, it is not, noted by wars and rumors of war. No, the self-developing nature of one's own soul has been manipulated by an unseen force, aka, the council of 300, to keep humankind from such development with said disharmony creating things. Such are the rumors of deception.

Can We the People rise up to the level of seeing and knowing this and take action on my proposal that will stop this anti-soul development that is, btw, in total harmony with the universe called source energy, and only dreamed about when the word God is used. My point is, that this is what is at stake, our very own soul. We are born into new lives all the time and only in a body are we able to process information that lets our soul develop into a "higher conscious" being. Keep in mind dear reader, that this subject is full of deceit and lies, so keep an open mind when venturing into the real truth, and gladly, we are not going there now, I just wanted to let you know where I stand on what the soul is, and what is at stake if we do not correct the constitution so that it can be self-correcting, wherein it like the human soul can be a self-generating force for good in our country and thereby be a light to the world.

The process of Suing the Gov for Breach of Contract

Since some of those in Gov are hell-bent on taking our freedom to even share ideas, claims, and allegations it is time we realize that this is a Breach of contract, one of many points of evidence, that we the people must now use to sue the gov as these abuses have gone on for many decades and we are at a persist, aka turning point, so we need to all wake up to what is actually going on in our country and world. This lawsuit will be the first step to order to implement the 4th Branch of Government, which will be set up by us, run by us, to keep the other three branches from staying away from its agreed-upon mission.

Come to think of it, I don't know the process as of this rendition on 9/29/2023 but you can rest assured if this gains momentum, we the people will figure it out. And in that case, our progress will be included here in future renditions of this book. Having said that the process is simple sounding, you find all the laws and legal opinions that became law surrounding this issue and use found information to file the suit in federal court, I suppose. My guess is the regional court who will bump it up to a more national court and it will take years. I will see about spending that up as many of you will want as well, too many crimes going on right now to delay in for even a single day, let alone the weeks and months we will soon hear it will take just to get a ruling on where to hear the case. I know, but it is our country so we have to love it no matter what right? Our love is our understanding, in this case, of how to fix things so patients we must have.

On that note, and to help the court, this plan is a two-fold process to get the 4th branch on the books and functional. The other is to get two new amendments added to the constitution that guides our country. Both efforts will be conducted at the same time so the breach lawsuit and the two amendments will play off each other in the media outlets to get into the national narrative, aka, so it can be talked about, and thought about by the general public. This we need more than anything else because I project, we will need 85% of the people behind and supporting this proposal in all its forms. So do share it, talk about it, find flaws in it, let's make it perfect and for our soul's sake and those of our young, let's get it done.

Okay, now let's take a break and see how our precious child we created in the lab of our mind, our government structure, is supposed to work.

Chapter Three

Are the Checks and Balances in Gov Flawed?

Yes, flawed in that it does not take into account massive corruption that is systemic in all three branches. The Second Amendment is a very weak and ineffective means be the government's self-correcting system. But the 4th branch as designed herein has at its heart, as its only mandate, to outlaw any harmful deception by the three branches of government and all its agencies as well as any corporation that serves the people with products to consume or use in some way.

I love the checks and balances means, but as any engineer will tell you, there is always a workaround to get the job done and if that job causes harm or is designed to cause harm to the un-wanting and unknowing public and that kind of loophole needs to be closed. That is really all that is missing, ok, well maybe add term limits in the House of Representatives. For the last 247 years, this country has been a nation it has tried to patch ways unscrupulous people have tried to make their profit earnings at the expense of the People and those patches have not worked because there was no solid power to let them succeed, there was always a workaround.

By ending harmful systemic deception, like we just learned from Rife's life story, which got into our health care system and caused all sorts of unhealthy situations, we can now end that kind of harmful deception cancer so the laws already on our books will have teeth and power to stop any further erosion of the state of our general welfare.

I ask you, what was put in place to ensure the Government always acts in the best interest of the people if the Three Branches become so corrupt that a change or alteration is in order? Most think it is the Second Amendment. Well as we can clearly see how the Second

Amendment is so extreme and fraught with ineffective results that we clearly need a new way.

The objective of having a three-way self-checking system of gov is to keep everyone honest when the debate, aka, talks about, the problems of the day that lead to solutions, take place. The debate system works when the ones participating are honorable men and women using accurate information about the components of the problem.

The banning of harmful deception has the best side effect of making every issue have one best solution above all others, that is what science-based thinking can do, get you to the best possible answer. This is how government can be made to run in the background unlike what it does today. We hang onto every word that comes from any action of anyone from the three branches. It must be some degree of fun but how did we get here? Seems so unnecessary. Even the heated debating would calm down due to the 4th Branch's high degree of work to supply the best truth there is so decisions would be made far easier and best for all concerned.

In a future rendition, this chapter will describe how the 3 Branches of the US Government work as we designed it, yes, having that one flaw of non-self-correcting by I figure 2% that has grown to be many times that in different branches and departments and agencies, some of which are 100% infected and have either lost their way or simply acting covertly letting no one know what they are doing, aka the black projects. So for now, let's hear the refreshing clarity of an AI, Chat GBT on the following title.

title: The Constitution's Checks and Balances: Safeguarding Honesty and Accountability in the United States

Introduction

The United States Constitution stands as a cornerstone of American governance, renowned for its ingenious system of checks and balances. Designed by the framers to prevent the concentration of power and ensure governmental accountability, this system has played a vital role in preserving honesty and integrity within the nation's governance. In this article, we will explore how the Constitution's checks and balances have served as a fundamental mechanism to keep everyone honest, from the executive to the legislative and judicial branches.

I. Separation of Powers

At the heart of the Constitution's system of checks and balances lies the principle of separation of powers. The framers recognized that the accumulation of power in a single branch would inevitably lead to corruption and tyranny. To prevent this, they divided governmental authority into three distinct branches: the executive, legislative, and judicial.

The executive branch, headed by the president, is responsible for executing laws and implementing policies. The legislative branch, comprising the Senate and the House of Representatives, enacts laws and controls the budget. The judicial branch, embodied by the Supreme Court and other federal courts, interprets the laws and ensures their constitutionality.

II. Executive Branch Oversight

To maintain honesty and accountability within the executive branch, the Constitution grants several checks and balances. First and foremost, the president's powers are limited and subject to the oversight of Congress. The legislative branch can impeach and remove a president for high crimes and misdemeanors, ensuring that the executive remains accountable to the people and the law.

Moreover, Congress exercises control over the budget, which serves as a significant check on executive actions. The president's proposed budget must undergo scrutiny and approval by Congress, allowing representatives to evaluate and restrict expenditures that may be deemed unnecessary or unwise.

III. Legislative Branch Checks

The Constitution empowers the legislative branch with several mechanisms to maintain honesty and accountability. Congress holds the authority to pass laws, but the president can veto them. However, Congress can override a presidential veto with a two-thirds majority vote in both houses, preventing the executive from unilaterally exerting power.

Furthermore, the Senate has the power to approve or reject presidential appointments, including those for federal judges and members of the executive branch. This confirmation process ensures that qualified and ethical individuals occupy key positions, promoting the principles of honesty and integrity in governance.

IV. Judicial Branch as the Arbiter

The judicial branch, guided by the Constitution, acts as a final arbiter and ensures the preservation of honesty and accountability. The Supreme Court has the authority to review the constitutionality of laws and executive actions. This power, known as judicial review, allows the Court to strike down laws that violate constitutional principles, preventing abuses of power and safeguarding individual rights.

Additionally, federal judges, including those in the Supreme Court, serve lifetime appointments to insulate them from political pressures. This independence ensures that judicial decisions are based on the merits of the law and constitutional interpretation rather than partisan biases, bolstering the integrity and fairness of the judicial system.

Conclusion

The Constitution's system of checks and balances stands as a testament to the framers' commitment to maintaining honesty and accountability within the United States government. By dividing power among the three branches and instituting checks on each other's authority, the Constitution ensures that no single entity becomes too powerful or unchecked. This delicate balance allows for the preservation of democratic values and serves as a fundamental mechanism to keep everyone honest, from the executive to the legislative and judicial branches, thus upholding the principles upon which the nation was founded.

Chapter Four

An incomplete list of those that were harmed by Deception in Gov or Biz or Both.

When JFK said: “Ask not what your country can do for you, ask what you can do for your country”. The following are those who followed his idea and did their best to help their country, the USA, but were thwarted by that very country’s Government. This is what must stop as it ruins our spirit of loving the light of creation.

This is where we talk about rife as the main example of breach of contract.

Rife is but one example, more recently there are claims and accusations of harmful deception in many areas that have affected our lives. Know that each and every one of these claims will be the last of their kind because harmful deception will end and the following stories will be for the history book.

We can also add the Amish have 90% fewer health problem

Add Glysophate: is in all our wheat-type floors, and ends up tearing holes in the gut: I know I need to cite sources for that claim.

The Founders of the US Constitution 50% of those who were ruined financially and some lost their lives due to British retaliation. They were powerless to stop the revolution and declaration of independence so they systematically destroyed the following.

Those who have been directly harmed by deception in the past are:

Politicians

John F. Kennedy; President: Tried to end deception within the government by using his words office and persuasive speech.

Robert F Kennedy, a Candidate waiting to be elected President: Implied he would continue his brother's cause, to end the deception in government.

Inventors

Nikola Tesla; inventor: Discoverer of many electromagnetic laws, tried to supply the earth with an abundance of electrical energy.

Royal Rife: inventor: Discovered exact frequency waves that could arrest all diseases in the body.

Wilhem Rich: inventor: Discovered how to control life force energy.

Billy Myers: inventor: Created the means to power an internal combustion engine with water.

Stefan Marinov: inventor: developed an over-unity motor.

John Mullen: inventor: Worked in black ops at MacDonald Douglas. Was working on projects designed to help humankind.

Dimitry Petronov: inventor, Developed a highly efficient plasma battery.

Zachary Warfield: inventor, Also developed a Plasma Battery.

Rory Johnson: Inventor, Cold fusion laser-activated magnetic motor that produced 500 hp called a magnetron motor. Died mysteriously.

Mark Tomion, Inventor, StarDrive propulsion engine.

Yuji Mulov: inventor, Made cold fusion a reality at far less cost.

Arie DeGeus: inventor: Patented the process of extracting zero-point energy from the field that is all around us.

Worry Johnson: inventor: Developed a cold fusion electric powered motor that made 500 hp.

Bruce DePalma: inventor: friend; Created an over-unity electric motor.

Mark Thomian: inventor: developed what he called a star drive for interstellar space travel

Whistle-Blowers

The Covid revelations See all the books written about how deception played a major roll in the whole incident.

Citizens

Big Biz The story of Glyphosate https://www.youtube.com/watch?v=5C2N5zcg19c

Dania Wigington, Reporting on Geo-Engineering, is the spraying of 502 yearly tons of chemicals in our skies what is causing weather harm including many of the extreme weather events? Seems to me his claims and evidence need an honest look because as he says loading the atmosphere with particulates is causing global warming by trapping the heat on Earth when the narrative does not even factor this into the equation.

To illustrate more thoroughly how the government has participated and controlled through deception an entire industry, that of health care. And to keep it simple we only need to look at one ruined life, that of Royal Rife.

I will cover this in detail in the next rendition of this, for now, know that his stellar work was so disruptive to the allopathic new form of medicine that the AMA was created to shut his methods down and prevent many more like it. This is the allegation that needs an honest review since Rife claimed and did demonstrate that he could kill cancer with his various frequencies generated by a machine making some sort of square wave impulse that affected any cell in the body. With cancer cells, he found the right frequencies for each one and vibrated them to their death. His celebration was short-lived however as those in charge of the country shut him down straight away, sadly for millions of We the People.

This is a story of where corporations conspired with the government to make our lives far worse than life had to be, going directly against the mission statement gov officials were sworn to uphold.

Chapter Five

Declaration for a 4th Branch of Government.
Declared July 4th 2023

I declare to you that we must add two new amendments to the US Constitution so that we may first restore our rightful place in the order of the whole nation granting us the right to vote for an amendment to be added to the Constitution, with another that outlaws using harmful deception by leaders in Business and Government.

We need to do this to fix a flaw, that of a lack of self-correcting government that apparently has infected many businesses, aka rich people. I ask you to consider supporting the 28th suggested amendment granting us this right to vote in a new amendment free from any congressional body or hackable voting machines (fyi, using a blockchain system that is publicly visible leaves no doubt to any vote, which far too many worry about), and the 29th which outlaws harmful deception conducted by any gov or biz organization that then can empower the creation of the 4th Branch to make sure there is swift action to stop all harmful deception used to influence decisions said groups make.

We need to do this since there are far too many allegations, claims, and proofs that the other 3 branches have been and are corrupted to an unknown degree, that We the People, now, do not fully trust our government and therefore we need to add these two amendments and empower the 4th Branch, created by We the People and will be totally run by We the People. It's sole purpose will be to make sure that deception does not happen and when it does we will take action to prove it is not true and move on or punish the one doing the harmful deceiving. More on how I see it being structured in Chapter 7.

Why now you ask, deception has been used forever, why outlaw what is human nature? Because it is not human nature in the slightest, it is learned behavior born of being hurt by someone older using it against them or some other pain, then since so many use it that hurt person uses it as one of their tools to avoid pain, and it goes on and on from there with each successful non facing the truth of the moment by deflecting into a lie to smooth things over. This is how we do it as an individual, which is not what the amendment is about at all, it is about when it is used to harm others, and in many cases, it has led to massive loss of life in almost any field of study you look.

Additionally, in order to make accurate decisions a person needs to base it on the truth, right, and in those that have the power to sell us products that could harm us in the long run, and those in power to dictate so many things in our life structure they need to base it on not lying to us as to the outcome of each decision. One bad decision at the foundation of a building can bring it to ruin and as a nation we cannot have that. We simply must realize these things, get fired up, and demand to allow the public to be able to vote for an amendment or two based on breach of contract and it is our right as who ordained the US Government structure into being we claim this right despite what the Constitution says in Article V:

The Congress, whenever two thirds of both Houses shall deem it necessary, shall propose Amendments to this Constitution, or, on the Application of the Legislatures of two-thirds of the several States, shall call a Convention for proposing Amendments, which, in either Case, shall be valid to all Intents and Purposes, as Part of this Constitution, when ratified by the Legislatures of three-fourths of the several States, or by Conventions in three fourths thereof, as the one or the other Mode of Ratification may be proposed by the Congress; Provided that no Amendment which may be made prior to the Year One thousand eight hundred and eight shall in any Manner affect the first and fourth Clauses in the Ninth Section of the first Article; and that no State, without its Consent, shall be deprived of its equal Suffrage in the Senate.

In normal human affairs, this would be an adequate guideline for any nation that has leaders fulfilling a preamble like our mission statement, but ours is not and the laws and regulations that try to correct corruption are not being enforced and thrown out of courts for weak reasons. So we will, as creators of the government guidelines need to take our rightful place at the head of the table, and as a nation of we the people and by 75% to 85% of the whole vote count, using an uncorrupted election process, vote for two new amendments to be added to our governments' guidelines into our sacred and original 1781 version of the Constitution.

Since harmful deception has been used by Biz and Gov for so long and it has brought us to many breaking points all at the same time then it is time to declare the need of a better form of checks and balances in our government structure as I have been saying. It is time for a 4th Branch to oversee the outcomes of the decisions the 3 branches make due to the outright abuse of authority of some in each and in the private sector.

Chapter Six

What is needed are two new amendments that Authorize the 4th Branch of Government.

To force the government and big business to stop harmful deceptive practices we will need to do the following.

1. Sue the U.S. Government for Breach of Contract. We can use the argument structure I laid out in Chapter 1.
2. At the same time start the national narrative to vote for and enact the 28th and 29th Amendments. Arrange for them to be voted on in the next national general election or as a stand-alone election using block-chain technology.
3. Once enacted pass a bill that allows for the creation of the 4th Branch of the U.S. Government and by popular vote choose its director in a subsequent election 30 days after the bill passes.
4. Put together the organization, aka, the 4th Branch, or the peoples' branch so that we can get back to creating a country for and by the people aimed at achieving its mission statement noted in the preamble.

To get all this done we the people must want it as a collective. Then we begin to harness the power of social media to let others know what we the people are doing and that they can join in the effort to correct what is wrong in our government. Who doesn't love our great nation enough to want to help this, to make sure that everyone who is making up the rules for us to live by has our best interest in the bill judgment ruling or executive order? We all do, so a lot more than others, and some that actually have it so well hidden within they tend to look like they do not care and only want destruction as if that was the way to fix things. I say no to anarchy and yes to a balance of powers. Listen, when this is fixed talking about the government will be a thing of the past because when right there is no need, all will be in order when deception is out of the equation.

This is an idea on how the 28th Amendment could be written. I asked an AI to write this up for us, both amendments, so both will need a rewrite by real constitution scholars.

Title: The Citizen-Led Amendment Act

Section 1: Purpose and Intent

The purpose of this Act is to establish a process by which the American people can propose and vote on new amendments to the United States Constitution. This measure aims to give citizens a direct role in shaping the nation's fundamental laws, while still respecting the constitutional framework and the balance of power established by the Constitution.

Section 2: The Amendment Initiative Process

(a) Any citizen of the United States, 18 years of age or older, may propose a new amendment to the Constitution by submitting a written copy of the proposed amendment, along with a petition containing the signatures of at least two percent of the eligible voters in a minimum of 38 states.

(b) Once a proposed amendment and petition have been submitted, the Congress shall have the authority to review the proposed amendment and to determine whether it is in compliance with the requirements of Article V of the Constitution.

(c) If the Congress chooses not to propose the amendment, it shall be placed on the national ballot for a vote during the next general election.

(d) A proposed amendment shall be ratified and become part of the Constitution if it is approved by a majority of voters in a minimum of 38 states.

Section 3: Limitations

(a) The Amendment Initiative process shall not be used to propose any amendment that would violate the basic principles of the Constitution, such as the protection of individual rights or the separation of powers.

(b) The Amendment Initiative process shall not be used to propose any amendment that would discriminate on the basis of race, sex, religion, or other protected characteristics.

(c) The Amendment Initiative process shall not be used to propose any amendment that would violate the equal protection clause or any other provision of the Constitution.

Section 4: Implementation

(a) The Congress shall have the authority to promulgate rules and regulations for the implementation of this Act, including but not limited to, the process for submitting proposed amendments and petitions, the procedure for reviewing proposed amendments, and the process for holding a national vote on proposed amendments.

(b) The Congress shall also have the authority to provide funding for the administration of the Amendment Initiative process.

(c) The Government shall carry out a public education campaign to inform citizens about the Amendment Initiative process and to provide resources for citizens to participate in the process.

Section 5: Separability

If any section or provision of this Act is held to be unconstitutional or invalid by a court of competent jurisdiction, such decision shall not affect the remaining sections or provisions of this Act.

This measure allows citizens to have a more direct role in the amendment process by enabling them to propose amendments through a petition process, without completely overriding the role of Congress. It establishes clear procedures and limitations for the proposal and voting process, and it also stipulates that it would not be used to infringe on individual rights, discrimination, or the equal protection clause.

And now for the meat of this effort, to add two more amendments to the US Constitution, the 29th, stop the lying by any government-serving official and corporation that sells products to We the People. To get us going in this write-up clarity before we send this to constitutional lawyers to look over, here is how writing research programmed writer put it.

This is an AI generated rough draft of how the 29th Amendment could be worded.

Title: The Truthful Information Disclosure Act

Section 1: Purpose and Intent

The purpose of this Act is to ensure that government and businesses provide accurate and truthful information to the public and their customers, in order to protect the rights of individuals and promote fair and honest business practices.

Section 2: Application

This Act applies to all government entities and businesses operating within the jurisdiction of the state, including but not limited to, federal, state, and local governments, corporations, partnerships, limited liability companies, and sole proprietorships.

Section 3: Prohibited Conduct

(a) Government entities and businesses shall not make any false or misleading statements or representations regarding their products, services, or any other matter, in any form of communication, including but not limited to, oral, written, or electronic forms that result in causing harm to anyone.

(b) Government entities and businesses shall not conceal, omit, or withhold any material information that is necessary to prevent any statement or representation made by them from being false or misleading.

(c) Government entities and businesses shall not use any deceptive or unfair practices, such as manipulation of data or statistics, in order to mislead the public or their customers.

Section 4: Enforcement and Penalties

(a) The state Attorney General, or a designee, shall have the authority to investigate and take legal action against any government entity or business that violates the provisions of this Act.

(b) Any government entity or business found to be in violation of this Act may be subject to fines, penalties, or other legal sanctions as determined by a court of law.

(c) Any individual or group of individuals who suffer a loss or injury as a result of a violation of this Act may also have the right to seek relief through a civil action.

Section 5: Public Education and Awareness

The state shall establish and maintain a public education and awareness program to inform the public about the provisions of this

Act and to provide resources for individuals to report suspected violations.

Section 6: Separability

If any section or provision of this Act is held to be unconstitutional or invalid by a court of competent jurisdiction, such decision shall not affect the remaining sections or provisions of this Act.

This law aims to establish clear and strict rules that prohibit our government and businesses from providing false or misleading information or hiding information to mislead the public and customers where the result in doing so has caused harm. It establishes the enforcement mechanism for the act, which is through the state attorney general's office and it provides penalties for the violation of the act. As well as it includes provisions for public education and awareness and provides a legal remedy for those who suffer losses as a result of false or misleading information.

It's important to note that while this law provides a framework for protecting the public from false or misleading information, it may not be able to fully prevent all forms of deception. Moreover, the complexity of some issues and data, and the subjectivity in interpreting them, can make it hard to fully enforce or prove a violation of the act. Therefore, a fully functional 4th Branch of our Government is suggested to be put in place to dig deeper into what is a fact or not. It is important that the act is enforced in a consistent and fair manner to minimize unintended consequences.

I know, such legal talk, makes one's head spin so much has to be done to keep people honest. Build one's inner sun and this never ever be an issue again by anyone. Reference is in the introduction to inner sun.

Chapter Seven

Objectives of the 4th Branch.

By the power of this proposed addition of the 29th Amendment to the U.S. Constitution, the 4th Branch of the U.S. Government can be created. Its task is to fulfill the 29th's Amendment goals which are to end harmful Deception as it affects any citizen of the United States.

I further propose that the structure or tasks that the 4th Branch will be responsible for are as follows:

1. To only be a responsive entity, that is it will only investigate harm created by deception brought to our attention by someone or entity with an evidence-based claim. It will never investigate such interactions on its own. In this way, it will fulfill the most important feature of the U.S. Constitution and that is to be by the people things get done and are for. So, to stop the deception from causing harm it will investigate claims by anyone and provide a rating on the subject.

2. I propose that the investigation will be performed with 3 steps: 1st; an open-source AI* will look over all the known data on the subject as reported by 3 different sources: A. Will be only peer-reviewed materials, B. will be all broadcasted info from Mainstream Media sources, and C. from all other media. The reports of these each will then be calculated into their respective category rating on a 100 to 1 scale as it is harmful deception or not. 2nd; The 4th Branch will then publish those results and open itself to any challenge to for accuracy by anyone. All counter-conclusions will be looked at and addressed to find the real truth. This will be done by a team of people who will study and look over everything carefully to come to a more accurate statement of truth on the issue. 3. If the issue gets to a 50/50 tie then the real non-bias science will be brought in to run tests and do repeatable

3. Experiments to find what is true, and with that known the level of harmful deception can be determined using the scale mentioned above.

4. After some or all of those three steps are completed then the rating of harmful deception can be published, used in a court of law, and by the power of the 29th amendment and the 4th Branch issue punishment recommendations.

5. Punishment recommendations will have guidelines ranging from days to one-year censorship, paying a fine, and/or jail time. Punishments are handed out when it is proven that the government or a corporation has harmed one person.

* What is meant by AI is a new system as yet to be properly named that will search the data banks of the world to find the best-known version of the truth. It will never be used as the final answer on anything, it is only used as a first step to weed out the obvious questions. It is only meant to serve as the first layer of study of to test a hypothesis or claim for accuracy. All answers generated for the public as part of its mission will come with sources so you can check to see how the answer was formulated. This will be done much like today's search engine we call 'Google' with the difference that it will not cater to outside influences, with the results listing conclusions with said three levels of depth as to what the truth is as each perspective has identified

I recommend that in order to determine deception and harm one must look at the situation being studied to determine if it fulfilled one or more of the six conditions in the preamble of the U.S. Constitution. They are:

1. Form a more perfect union = form a nation from a collection of sovereign states where all co-operate with each other.

2. Establish Justice = make fair all laws and judgments to the accused.

3. Ensure domestic tranquility = create peace within our union noted by the smooth operation of the government and biz.

4. Provide the common defense = secure our borders against all invaders.

5. Promote general welfare = promote good health to all.

6. Secure the blessings of liberty to ourselves and our posterity = which means the government will protect our freedoms called liberty as a sovereign nation as a timeless endevor.

The rules would be that if any issue was 100% harmful deception in any one of these six goals, then the rating would be 100% Harmful Deception, not one-sixth Harmful Deception on the reasoning that it was not harmful in five of six so it is not all that bad. No, the condition is harm, 100% of people died, were maimed, ruined, you name the harm, it happened and it was a 100% cause of such harm.

Since hereafter no one will be able to deceive another that causes harm, this new 4th branch will have an elected person run it. We the people shall elect him or her and the person shall be answerable, as in, kept in check, by anyone from the three branches of the current government.

So, let's do this. There will be many steps along the way as we will soon see, just know that this new branch will be what the founders wanted and intended by adding the 2nd Amendment, they just did not know the details of the problem at the time and there for did not know how to add the appropriate self-correcting means to do so.

More can be said on how to structure the 4th Branch's mission and that will be done in future editions.

Chapter Eight

How We the People can get it done

The creation of a 4th Branch of government to keep in check the other three branches will be a herculean effort because it involves waking people up to the real facts of how the government has not served its people well and failed globally in its strong-arm tactics. This has resulted in a breach of the mission it agrees to every time a newly elected official takes office as the preamble to the US Constitution states. So how do We the People become united with this mission, to keep the Government honest in keeping the goals of the government of the United States on track so its served people can thrive as planned?

Today there are more tools than ever to transmit a message so that is how we get this needed project going thereby creating it. Here is a list of things I can think of doing right now and with a timeline of milestones completed.

Milestone list of things to get done

1. Argue that the US Constitution is a contract as part of a trial, a documentary proving as this book suggests, a breach of contract has occurred, advance this proposal via interviews on social media, make a YouTube channel called AweWay which combines the means of the Trinity Balance Formula to find the truth which is how to create Awe within you. This too will be the goal of the 4th Branch, to create within a real sense of the feeling and knowing of Awe by knowing the truth. We will focus on this instead of all the contentious and conflicting results of decisions have on people that is so unnecessary.

2. Doing milestone one will add this proposal to the national narrative so that the two amendments can be voted on by We the People. This will feel like the hundredth monkey effect

3. has kicked in when everyone is suddenly talking about it. I look forward to this day.

4. Getting both amendments on the ballot in all 50 States in a legal referendum to be voted on by the 75% of the people.

5. Once both pass then by the self-authorizing of the 19th amendment the 4th branch can be created. A team of people will come together to begin organizing the parts necessary to give the 4th Branch the right paper work, resources to investigate claims of deception, and proper legal documents to punish the offenders as it responds to the publics complains of what harmful deception has affected them. A special or regular election will be held to pick the head of the 4th branch as soon as possible.

At the time of this writing, I only have my personal Facebook page to talk with people. I will need to get a telegram channel and a YouTube channel called AweWay to have as its focus the Trinity Balance Formula of Wholeness solutions with this project being the first one covered. As it grows, I will do live shows so we can get to more solutions to current problems as this one, the 4th Branch will not cover all problems in the world that this formula is claimed to be able to solve.

Once my channel on YouTube gets going then it will be time for interviews with the main thought leaders and influencers of our day. I want to go to the thought leaders that are helping shape the future by not only exposing the real truths of the day but have solutions that are reasonable and doable.

It is my hope that these thought leaders will see this book's argument as reasonable and doable as well as highly needed at this time due to the proposed higher levels of control, tracking, monitoring, higher taxes to pay for it, more unwanted wars, more hiding the real truths as chapter 4 highlighted and more. And when they do get it and support it the snowball will have been built, then we can carefully let everyone know all about it via this book, the influencers, the celebrities, and even some political types will get on board and surprise us.

But it will mostly grow with you, the reader, who knows what is being proposed, a real way to regain in an out-of-control government without bloodshed, without confusion, and with the least amount of resistance one could ever hope for. So vote for the 28th and 29th Amendments when you see them on your national ballot. Write a book on this too if you feel it will help. I know right now it feels like David Vs Goliath but with your help, we can change that balance of power. I suspect for many coming to the understanding in this book's proposal will be like waking up from a dream, a bad dream. So, look into helping this proposal at some point because We the People, sharing this needed solution to hold our elected officials and corporations accountable for advancing their cause using deception that has harmed us, simply have to stop it, how many more have to die, be maned, forced into such controlled thinking that freedom of spirit is lost?

Another step we can take is to record all the insistences of deception that have led to harming any number of We the People. So, send in your reports so they can be added to the Breach of Contract rial We the People will bring against our government and Corporations all sworn one way or another to not cause harm to We the People.

Chapter Nine

Comments from We the People

Kathy Katz

Absolutely brilliant idea and the project you have come up with to add 2 new Amendment to the constitution that would STOP and PROHIBIT all the lying, misinformation, and misrepresentation of products and services that government entities, corporations, businesses, etc. are heavily engaged in in in against We, the People.

The current root cause of all the suffering in the world is a direct result of the power, We, the People, have given them and which they have abused to a level never seen before and that is beyond belief. Allowing them to continue to mislead and deceive us without any repercussion means we are allowing them to literally get away with murder.

This misuse of power must be addressed, changed, and eliminated and they must be held accountable for all violations of deception against Humanity.
Your proposal to create a fourth agency of people who will not succumb to bribery to maintain checks and balances and administer punishment to those who violate the truth in any fashion is yet another great idea.

Can you imagine living in a world where we could trust our government entities, corporations, and businesses, the end of fake news and products and services we could trust that were not hiding any hidden dangers to our health and well-being????

We the people, can take back our power through these two proposed Constitutional Amendments, or else this shit show will only continue and ultimately contribute to our demise.

The only way this shit show survives is through LIES therefore a new Amendment, submitted by We the People, prohibiting lying from said agencies along with punishment for violation absolutely needs to be implemented.

I think your proposal is laser-on-point and hope more people jump on this bandwagon and bring it to fruition.

IMO, Your article on solutions to our current dilemma nails it !!!! It cuts the head of the snake off and is a great starting point to bring Heaven to Earth.

And from Joesph Zenner

As time has elapsed in this country, a need has developed for a way to get to the actual truth. "Fact checkers" for social media sites have been shown to be wrong more than they are correct. The mainstream media has become a haven of Mis and disinformation and obviously politicians are compromised. This puts us in a space where getting to the actual truth of a matter has become increasingly difficult. That is why I was thrilled to see Mr Longo's proposal to create a 4th branch of government that can help us find a way to get to the truth of important topics. I find his approach to this to be both innovative and impressive. I hope we can create the support to turn this into a reality.

Chapter Ten

Pros, Cons and other thoughts on this Plan.

Pros

With this one simple addition to the Constitution, we fix pretty much everything that is limiting our country to be perfect, to be all it can be, be a place where we the people can thrive including those persons in Gov which is a huge part of the tax paying public.

Makes the distinction between a harmless lie and harmful deception, a huge part of how humans play with each other testing their psychic skills.

Would stop the extreme efforts corporations make to bend the laws for profit.

Would stop process food manufactures from putting poison in our food supply. Same with water companies. We want live food and water, live because it supports life and does not dimmish it.

Would grow many businesses designed to replace a failed or weak part of our economy namely food and medicine production.

Takes the burden off Congress people by finally being able to trust information anyone is giving them or they find in their research efforts. They will have access like anyone else to research the data real truth is based on that the 4th Branch will use.

Thoughts from others. Many know there is something very wrong with the way the U.S. Government operates by studying the results of its actions and many say to make a today new government structure. To these people I ask you to look at this one single yet major addition to the system we call the U.S. Government. We shall use the fail-safe of honesty and sincere enforceable holding to account focus on fulfilling the 6 pre amble goals for our Nation. The hidden goal is that we would be the light for all nations to strive for as we actually did achieve some decades back. We don't need a new structure for the government if it would simply use truthful information to then be able to decide and issue. That would do it as it has in long trials in our past with our current laws, but now, in this information age, we need to shorten the time from claimed deception causing harm to its cessation. We need the power of enforcing the cessation of harmful deceptive behavior so those that make the decisions will have the correct info to go by. I will suggest that all three steps are completed by the 4th branch before making its percent of harmful deception ruling as Chapter Sevens outline.

I propose to make this 4th Branch completely self-sufficient by creating the AI type search engine to look on 3 levels of data that has a say as to what is true. Then as it is offered to the public for free to use all of will be paid for by adds we let market with us, much like the way Google does biz, or FB for that matter. The 3 levels it will study to formulate its best answer are professional peer reviewed papers, Main stream media sources, and all other sources of opinion or facts on an issue in question.

Outlaw lying and deception that causing harm and Journalists can get back to honest journalism, digging for the right facts. The 4th Branch will help them.

Cons

The effect of ending sales of harmful, deceptive produced, products will cause a reduction in sales tax on products which is mostly a state loss. I will have to look into what kind of losses would occur when products like round up are never used again on American soil in terms of economic loss of jobs and company income where the Fed and State also has a gain. Earth worms have been all but destroyed in Americas farm lands due to farming practices of using pest killing glyphosate fertilizers, and plowing without worms the crops we grow have far fewer nutrients which is the very line crossed that defines harm. We need our earth worms back, so now we see the plus side of that.

Many other products will be eliminated from store shelves but that is not something bad as companies will simply adject the ingredients to not be harmful to us. We are in the business of thrive, each and every one of us so to make anything that gets in the way of that is so last century, to make a joke. But what is two centuries ago is the stated goal of our country and that is to produce and environment for We the People to thrive. I think we have seen enough of how things do not work, so now is a good time to flip the switch and get back to basics, get back to fulfilling the U.S. Constitution's pre amble mission statement. Yes, now is a good time.

Now let's take a closer look at what We the People will positively get from the functional 4th Branch of the U.S. Government.

Chapter Eleven

What we will get for doing this?

So, after all the effort to legally add two amendments to the U.S. Constitution, thereby authorizing a 4th Branch of government to eliminate harmful deception, what do we get out of it? Fair question and that is to be expected by those that begin reading here, lol.

What we get is a government working to stay in the background while fulfilling its duty to helping those in the United States of America obtain all six promises in the preamble: 1 to form a more perfect union, 2 to establish justice, 3 insure domestic tranquility, 4 provide for the common defense (not offense), 5 promote the general welfare, and 6 secure this achievement in liberty for all generations to come.

We get to stop anything that does not live up to these ends because we know then that they were created using deception, example the reason to fight with Iraq was all made up, with no reality to it costs how many lives and expenses, all needless where resources could have gone to more supportive projects, or not at all and paid down our debt.

We get to know our government is working on our behalf and can rest in that. This produces peace of mind that you will treasure to no end which in turn will cause you to thrive and be free of limiting type thinking.

We get to know we began a legal movement that will transform the world into truth seekers as we again become that shining light upon the hill.

We get to know that with the ending of deception this will be done more efficiently and thereby reduces cost to the Government by some per cent (10 to 30%) as to be determined with each program then showing the total average savings over all.

I know many of you have something to say about what our benefits will be so please send them in and I will include them with your name if you like here. Just know this would be such a long list due to the massive voiding of contracts that were agreed to under duress.

Conclusion

This is our fight, We the People, so I ask each and every one of you to make this your own fight by any means you think right as you have the time and inclination. We simply must stop harmful deception by those that we trust to lead us with law-making, public policies, and selling products to us, aka, the means of this proposal. We can suggest voting for this to our friends, writing letters, talking to larger groups, voting for it on the day it is on the ballot, and making a donation of time and or money to help it along. I will use all proceeds from this work to do the same pay for all I can as there will be expenses.

In any case, we need to make this a big part of the national narrative. We need to fix the system by adding a layer of self-checking to all the things gov and biz do in regard to the six mission statement goals in our constitution's preamble that specifically aim at creating conditions where we can thrive as people. I would only add our thriving does not conflict with nature in any way, but that is for policymakers to create the conditions for and is not in the realm of powers of the proposed 4th branch. It is only designed to stop harm due to deception by the government and corporations that sell to the public.

People cannot make accurate decisions with inaccurate facts; our recent pandemic has made that very clear to anyone who has been paying attention. My bet is if you trace back to the cause of all problems that our government has had a hand in you'll find deception occurred at a key point in the decision process. The same will be found in corporations that sold us poisonous concoctions, and/or delayed or stopped health-giving solutions.

Deception is the enemy of all sane people. We hired all these entities to serve us and they failed to one degree or another so now it is time to put an end to this as we approach many new things such as AI and the singularity, coming from a place where many nations will not even take our food imports it is that bad. The word is getting out about how harmful things have been done to us with the full awareness of the few over the many. I hope you join this fight and creation, never before is it more needed than now.

As always, let me know what you think needs to be added to this or subtracted. Help me make this as good an argument as it can be.

Appendix A

Our Three Founding Documents

Declaration of Independence Declared on July 4th 1776

The unanimous Declaration of the thirteen United States of America, When in the Course of human events, it becomes necessary for one people to dissolve the political bands which have connected them with another, and to assume among the powers of the earth, the separate and equal station to which the Laws of Nature and of Nature's God entitle them, a decent respect to the opinions of mankind requires that they should declare the causes which impel them to the separation.

We hold these truths to be self-evident, that all men are created equal, that they are endowed by their Creator with certain unalienable Rights, that among these are Life, Liberty and the pursuit of Happiness.--That to secure these rights, Governments are instituted among Men, deriving their just powers from the consent of the governed, --That whenever any Form of Government becomes destructive of these ends, it is the Right of the People to alter or to abolish it, and to institute new Government, laying its foundation on such principles and organizing its powers in such form, as to them shall seem most likely to effect their Safety and Happiness. Prudence, indeed, will dictate that Governments long established should not be changed for light and transient causes; and accordingly, all experience hath shewn, that mankind are more disposed to suffer, while evils are sufferable than to right themselves by abolishing the forms to which they are accustomed. But when a long train of abuses and usurpations, pursuing invariably the same Object evinces a design to reduce them under absolute Despotism, it is their right, it is their duty, to throw off such Government, and to provide new Guards for their future security. Such has been the patient sufferance of these Colonies; and such is now the necessity which constrains them to alter their former Systems of Government. The history of the present King of Great Britain is a history of repeated injuries and usurpations, all having in direct object the establishment of an absolute Tyranny over these States. To prove this, let Facts be submitted to a candid world.

He has refused his Assent to Laws, the most wholesome and necessary for the public good.

He has forbidden his Governors to pass Laws of immediate and pressing importance unless suspended in their operation till his Assent should be obtained; and when so suspended, he has utterly neglected to attend to them.

He has refused to pass other Laws for the accommodation of large districts of people, unless those people would relinquish the right of Representation in the Legislature, a right inestimable to them and formidable to tyrants only.

He has called together legislative bodies at places unusual, uncomfortable, and distant from the depository of their public Records, for the sole purpose of fatiguing them into compliance with his measures.

He has dissolved Representative Houses repeatedly, for opposing with manly firmness his invasions on the rights of the people.

He has refused for a long time, after such dissolutions, to cause others to be elected; whereby the Legislative powers, incapable of Annihilation, have returned to the People at large for their exercise; the State remaining in the mean time exposed to all the dangers of invasion from without, and convulsions within.

He has endeavored to prevent the population of these States; for that purpose obstructing the Laws for Naturalization of Foreigners;

refusing to pass others to encourage their migrations hither, and raising the conditions of new Appropriations of Lands.

He has obstructed the Administration of Justice, by refusing his Assent to Laws for establishing Judiciary powers.

He has made Judges dependent on his Will alone, for the tenure of their offices, and the amount and payment of their salaries.

He has erected a multitude of New Offices, and sent hither swarms of Officers to harrass our people, and eat out their substance.

He has kept among us, in times of peace, Standing Armies without the Consent of our legislatures.

He has affected to render the Military independent of and superior to the Civil power.

He has combined with others to subject us to a jurisdiction foreign to our constitution, and unacknowledged by our laws; giving his Assent to their Acts of pretended Legislation:

For Quartering large bodies of armed troops among us:

For protecting them, by a mock Trial, from punishment for any Murders which they should commit on the Inhabitants of these States:

For cutting off our Trade with all parts of the world:

For imposing Taxes on us without our Consent:

For depriving us in many cases, of the benefits of Trial by Jury:

For transporting us beyond Seas to be tried for pretended offenses

For abolishing the free System of English Laws in a neighboring Province, establishing therein an Arbitrary government, and enlarging its Boundaries so as to render it at once an example and fit instrument for introducing the same absolute rule into these Colonies:

For taking away our Charters, abolishing our most valuable Laws, and altering fundamentally the Forms of our Governments:

For suspending our own Legislatures, and declaring themselves invested with power to legislate for us in all cases whatsoever.

He has abdicated Government here, by declaring us out of his Protection and waging War against us.

He has plundered our seas, ravaged our Coasts, burnt our towns, and destroyed the lives of our people.

He is at this time transporting large Armies of foreign Mercenaries to complete the works of death, desolation and tyranny, already begun with circumstances of Cruelty & perfidy scarcely paralleled in the most barbarous ages, and totally unworthy the Head of a civilized nation.

He has constrained our fellow Citizens taken Captive on the high Seas to bear Arms against their Country, to become the executioners of their friends and Brethren, or to fall themselves by their Hands.

He has excited domestic insurrections amongst us, and has endeavored to bring on the inhabitants of our frontiers, the merciless Indian Savages, whose known rule of warfare, is an undistinguished destruction of all ages, sexes and conditions.

In every stage of these Oppressions We have Petitioned for Redress in the most humble terms: Our repeated Petitions have been answered only by repeated injury. A Prince whose character is thus marked by every act which may define a Tyrant, is unfit to be the ruler of a free people.

Nor have We been wanting in attentions to our British brethren. We have warned them from time to time of attempts by their legislature to extend an unwarrantable jurisdiction over us. We have reminded them of the circumstances of our emigration and settlement here. We have appealed to their native justice and magnanimity, and we have conjured them by the ties of our common kindred to disavow these usurpations, which, would inevitably interrupt our connections and correspondence. They too have been deaf to the voice of justice and of consanguinity. We must, therefore, acquiesce in the necessity, which denounces our Separation, and hold them, as we hold the rest of mankind, Enemies in War, in Peace Friends.

We, therefore, the Representatives of the United States of America, in General Congress, Assembled, appealing to the Supreme Judge of the world for the rectitude of our intentions, do, in the Name, and by Authority of the good People of these Colonies, solemnly publish and declare, That these United Colonies are, and of Right ought to be Free and Independent States; that they are Absolved from all Allegiance to the British Crown, and that all political connection between them and the State of Great Britain, is and ought to be totally dissolved; and that as Free and Independent States, they have full Power to levy War, conclude Peace, contract Alliances, establish Commerce, and to do all other Acts and Things which Independent States may of right do. And for the support of this Declaration, with a firm reliance on the protection of divine Providence, we mutually pledge to each other our Lives, our Fortunes and our sacred Honor.

Those who signed it. I will say a few words on each asap.
Georgia

Button Gwinnett

Lyman Hall

George Walton

North Carolina

William Hooper

Joseph Hewes

John Penn

South Carolina

Edward Rutledge

Thomas Heyward, Jr.

Thomas Lynch, Jr.

Arthur Middleton

Massachusetts

John Hancock

Maryland

Samuel Chase

William Paca

Thomas Stone

Charles Carroll of Carrollton

Virginia

George Wythe

Richard Henry Lee

Thomas Jefferson

Benjamin Harrison

Thomas Nelson, Jr.

Francis Lightfoot Lee

Carter Braxton

Pennsylvania

Robert Morris

Benjamin Rush

Benjamin Franklin

John Morton

George Clymer

James Smith

George Taylor

James Wilson

George Ross

Delaware

Caesar Rodney

George Read

Thomas McKean

New York

William Floyd

Philip Livingston

Francis Lewis

Lewis Morris

New Jersey

Richard Stockton

John Witherspoon

Francis Hopkinson

John Hart

Abraham Clark

New Hampshire

Josiah Bartlett

William Whipple

Massachusetts

Samuel Adams

John Adams

Robert Treat Paine

Elbridge Gerry

Rhode Island

Stephen Hopkins

William Ellery

Connecticut

Roger Sherman

Samuel Huntington

William Williams

Oliver Wolcott

New Hampshire

Matthew Thornton

The US Constitution ratified on May 29, 1790

We the People of the United States, in Order to form a more perfect Union, establish Justice, insure domestic Tranquility, provide for the common defence, promote the general Welfare, and secure the Blessings of Liberty to ourselves and our Posterity, do ordain and establish this Constitution for the United States of America.

Article. I.

Section. 1.
All legislative Powers herein granted shall be vested in a Congress of the United States, which shall consist of a Senate and House of Representatives.

Section. 2.
The House of Representatives shall be composed of Members chosen every second Year by the People of the several States, and the Electors in each State shall have the Qualifications requisite for Electors of the most numerous Branch of the State Legislature.

No Person shall be a Representative who shall not have attained to the Age of twenty five Years, and been seven Years a Citizen of the United States, and who shall not, when elected, be an Inhabitant of that State in which he shall be chosen.

Representatives and direct Taxes shall be apportioned among the several States which may be included within this Union, according to their respective Numbers, which shall be determined by adding to the whole Number of free Persons, including those bound to Service for a Term of Years, and excluding Indians not taxed, three fifths of all other Persons. The actual Enumeration shall be made within three Years after the first Meeting of the Congress of the United States, and within every subsequent Term of ten Years, in such Manner as they shall by Law direct. The Number of Representatives shall not exceed one for every thirty Thousand, but each State shall have at Least one Representative; and until such enumeration shall be made, the State of New Hampshire shall be entitled to chuse three, Massachusetts eight, Rhode-Island and Providence Plantations one, Connecticut five, New-York six, New Jersey four, Pennsylvania eight, Delaware one, Maryland six, Virginia ten, North Carolina five, South Carolina five, and Georgia three.

When vacancies happen in the Representation from any State, the Executive Authority thereof shall issue Writs of Election to fill such Vacancies.

The House of Representatives shall chuse their Speaker and other Officers; and shall have the sole Power of Impeachment.

Section. 3.

The Senate of the United States shall be composed of two Senators from each State, chosen by the Legislature thereof, for six Years; and each Senator shall have one Vote.

Immediately after they shall be assembled in Consequence of the first Election, they shall be divided as equally as may be into three Classes. The Seats of the Senators of the first Class shall be vacated at the Expiration of the second Year, of the second Class at the Expiration of the fourth Year, and of the third Class at the Expiration of the sixth Year, so that one third may be chosen every second Year; and if Vacancies happen by Resignation, or otherwise, during the Recess of the Legislature of any State, the Executive thereof may make temporary Appointments until the next Meeting of the Legislature, which shall then fill such Vacancies.

No Person shall be a Senator who shall not have attained to the Age of thirty Years, and been nine Years a Citizen of the United States, and who shall not, when elected, be an Inhabitant of that State for which he shall be chosen.

The Vice President of the United States shall be President of the Senate, but shall have no Vote, unless they be equally divided.

The Senate shall chuse their other Officers, and also a President pro tempore, in the Absence of the Vice President, or when he shall exercise the Office of President of the United States.

The Senate shall have the sole Power to try all Impeachments. When sitting for that Purpose, they shall be on Oath or Affirmation. When the President of the United States is tried, the Chief Justice shall preside: And no Person shall be convicted without the Concurrence of two thirds of the Members present.

Judgment in Cases of Impeachment shall not extend further than to removal from Office, and disqualification to hold and enjoy any Office of honor, Trust or Profit under the United States: but the Party convicted shall nevertheless be liable and subject to Indictment, Trial, Judgment and Punishment, according to Law.

Section. 4.
The Times, Places and Manner of holding Elections for Senators and Representatives, shall be prescribed in each State by the Legislature thereof; but the Congress may at any time by Law make or alter such Regulations, except as to the Places of chusing Senators.

The Congress shall assemble at least once in every Year, and such Meeting shall be on the first Monday in December, unless they shall by Law appoint a different Day.

Section. 5.
Each House shall be the Judge of the Elections, Returns and Qualifications of its own Members, and a Majority of each shall constitute a Quorum to do Business; but a smaller Number may adjourn from day to day, and may be authorized to compel the Attendance of absent Members, in such Manner, and under such Penalties as each House may provide.

Each House may determine the Rules of its Proceedings, punish its Members for disorderly Behaviour, and, with the Concurrence of two-thirds, expel a Member.

Each House shall keep a Journal of its Proceedings, and from time to time publish the same, excepting such Parts as may in their Judgment require Secrecy; and the Yeas and Nays of the Members of either House on any question shall, at the Desire of one fifth of those Present, be entered on the Journal.

Neither House, during the Session of Congress, shall, without the Consent of the other, adjourn for more than three days, nor to any other Place than that in which the two Houses shall be sitting.

Section. 6.
The Senators and Representatives shall receive a Compensation for their Services, to be ascertained by Law, and paid out of the Treasury of the United States. They shall in all Cases, except Treason, Felony and Breach of the Peace, be privileged from Arrest during their Attendance at the Session of their respective Houses, and in going to and returning from the same; and for any Speech or Debate in either House, they shall not be questioned in any other Place.

No Senator or Representative shall, during the Time for which he was elected, be appointed to any civil Office under the Authority of the United States, which shall have been created, or the Emoluments whereof shall have been encreased during such time; and no Person holding any Office under the United States, shall be a Member of either House during his Continuance in Office.

Section. 7.
All Bills for raising Revenue shall originate in the House of Representatives; but the Senate may propose or concur with Amendments as on other Bills.

Every Bill which shall have passed the House of Representatives and the Senate, shall, before it become a Law, be presented to the President of the United States; If he approve he shall sign it, but if not he shall return it, with his Objections to that House in which it shall have originated, who shall enter the Objections at large on their Journal, and proceed to reconsider it. If after such Reconsideration two thirds of that House shall agree to pass the Bill, it shall be sent, together with the Objections, to the other House, by which it shall likewise be reconsidered, and if approved by two thirds of that House, it shall become a Law. But in all such Cases the Votes of both Houses shall be determined by yeas and Nays, and the Names of the Persons voting for and against the Bill shall be entered on the Journal of each House respectively. If any

Bill shall not be returned by the President within ten Days (Sundays excepted) after it shall have been presented to him, the Same shall be a Law, in like Manner as if he had signed it, unless the Congress by their Adjournment prevent its Return, in which Case it shall not be a Law.

Every Order, Resolution, or Vote to which the Concurrence of the Senate and House of Representatives may be necessary (except on a question of Adjournment) shall be presented to the President of the United States; and before the Same shall take Effect, shall be approved by him, or being disapproved by him, shall be repassed by two thirds of the Senate and House of Representatives, according to the Rules and Limitations prescribed in the Case of a Bill.

Section. 8.

The Congress shall have Power To lay and collect Taxes, Duties, Imposts and Excises, to pay the Debts and provide for the common Defence and general Welfare of the United States; but all Duties, Imposts and Excises shall be uniform throughout the United States;

To borrow Money on the credit of the United States;

To regulate Commerce with foreign Nations, and among the several States, and with the Indian Tribes;

To establish an uniform Rule of Naturalization, and uniform Laws on the subject of Bankruptcies throughout the United States;

To coin Money, regulate the Value thereof, and of foreign Coin, and fix the Standard of Weights and Measures;

To provide for the Punishment of counterfeiting the Securities and current Coin of the United States;

To establish Post Offices and post Roads;

To promote the Progress of Science and useful Arts, by securing for limited Times to Authors and Inventors the exclusive Right to their respective Writings and Discoveries;

To constitute Tribunals inferior to the Supreme Court;

To define and punish Piracies and Felonies committed on the high Seas, and Offences against the Law of Nations;

To declare War, grant Letters of Marque and Reprisal, and make Rules concerning Captures on Land and Water;

To raise and support Armies, but no Appropriation of Money to that Use shall be for a longer Term than two Years;

To provide and maintain a Navy;

To make Rules for the Government and Regulation of the land and naval Forces;

To provide for calling forth the Militia to execute the Laws of the Union, suppress Insurrections and repel Invasions;

To provide for organizing, arming, and disciplining, the Militia, and for governing such Part of them as may be employed in the Service of the United States, reserving to the States respectively, the Appointment of the Officers, and the Authority of training the Militia according to the discipline prescribed by Congress;

To exercise exclusive Legislation in all Cases whatsoever, over such District (not exceeding ten Miles square) as may, by Cession of particular States, and the Acceptance of Congress, become the Seat of the Government of the United States, and to exercise like Authority over all Places purchased by the Consent of the Legislature of the State in which the Same shall be, for the Erection of Forts, Magazines, Arsenals, dock-Yards, and other needful Buildings;—And

To make all Laws which shall be necessary and proper for carrying into Execution the foregoing Powers, and all other Powers vested by this Constitution in the Government of the United States, or in any Department or Officer thereof.

Section. 9.
The Migration or Importation of such Persons as any of the States now existing shall think proper to admit, shall not be prohibited by the Congress prior to the Year one thousand eight hundred and eight, but a Tax or duty may be imposed on such Importation, not exceeding ten dollars for each Person.

The Privilege of the Writ of Habeas Corpus shall not be suspended, unless when in Cases of Rebellion or Invasion the public Safety may require it.

No Bill of Attainder or ex post facto Law shall be passed.

No Capitation, or other direct, Tax shall be laid, unless in Proportion to the Census or enumeration herein before directed to be taken.

No Tax or Duty shall be laid on Articles exported from any State.

No Preference shall be given by any Regulation of Commerce or Revenue to the Ports of one State over those of another: nor shall Vessels bound to, or from, one State, be obliged to enter, clear, or pay Duties in another.

No Money shall be drawn from the Treasury, but in Consequence of Appropriations made by Law; and a regular Statement and Account of the Receipts and Expenditures of all public Money shall be published from time to time.

No Title of Nobility shall be granted by the United States: And no Person holding any Office of Profit or Trust under them, shall, without the Consent of the Congress, accept of any present, Emolument, Office, or Title, of any kind whatever, from any King, Prince, or foreign State.

Section. 10.
No State shall enter into any Treaty, Alliance, or Confederation; grant Letters of Marque and Reprisal; coin Money; emit Bills of Credit; make any Thing but gold and silver Coin a Tender in

Payment of Debts; pass any Bill of Attainder, ex post facto Law, or Law impairing the Obligation of Contracts, or grant any Title of Nobility.

No State shall, without the Consent of the Congress, lay any Imposts or Duties on Imports or Exports, except what may be absolutely necessary for executing it's inspection Laws: and the net Produce of all Duties and Imposts, laid by any State on Imports or Exports, shall be for the Use of the Treasury of the United States; and all such Laws shall be subject to the Revision and Controul of the Congress.

No State shall, without the Consent of Congress, lay any Duty of Tonnage, keep Troops, or Ships of War in time of Peace, enter into any Agreement or Compact with another State, or with a foreign Power, or engage in War, unless actually invaded, or in such imminent Danger as will not admit of delay.

Article. II.

Section. 1.

The executive Power shall be vested in a President of the United States of America. He shall hold his Office during the Term of four Years, and, together with the Vice President, chosen for the same Term, be elected, as follows

Each State shall appoint, in such Manner as the Legislature thereof may direct, a Number of Electors, equal to the whole Number of Senators and Representatives to which the State may be entitled in the Congress: but no Senator or Representative, or Person holding an Office of Trust or Profit under the United States, shall be appointed an Elector.

The Electors shall meet in their respective States, and vote by Ballot for two Persons, of whom one at least shall not be an Inhabitant of the same State with themselves. And they shall make a List of all the Persons voted for, and of the Number of Votes for each; which List they shall sign and certify, and transmit sealed to the Seat of the Government of the United States, directed to the President of the Senate. The President of the Senate shall, in the Presence of the

Senate and House of Representatives, open all the Certificates, and the Votes shall then be counted. The Person having the greatest Number of Votes shall be the President, if such Number be a Majority of the whole Number of Electors appointed; and if there be more than one who have such Majority, and have an equal Number of Votes, then the House of Representatives shall immediately chuse by Ballot one of them for President; and if no Person have a Majority, then from the five highest on the List the said House shall in like Manner chuse the President. But in chusing the President, the Votes shall be taken by States, the Representation from each State having one Vote; A quorum for this Purpose shall consist of a Member or Members from two thirds of the States, and a Majority of all the States shall be necessary to a Choice. In every Case, after the Choice of the President, the Person having the greatest Number of Votes of the Electors shall be the Vice President. But if there should remain two or more who have equal Votes, the Senate shall chuse from them by Ballot the Vice President.

The Congress may determine the Time of chusing the Electors, and the Day on which they shall give their Votes; which Day shall be the same throughout the United States.

No Person except a natural born Citizen, or a Citizen of the United States, at the time of the Adoption of this Constitution, shall be eligible to the Office of President; neither shall any Person be eligible to that Office who shall not have attained to the Age of thirty five Years, and been fourteen Years a Resident within the United States.

In Case of the Removal of the President from Office, or of his Death, Resignation, or Inability to discharge the Powers and Duties of the said Office, the Same shall devolve on the Vice President, and the Congress may by Law provide for the Case of Removal, Death, Resignation or Inability, both of the President and Vice President, declaring what Officer shall then act as President, and such Officer shall act accordingly, until the Disability be removed, or a President shall be elected.

The President shall, at stated Times, receive for his Services, a Compensation, which shall neither be encreased nor diminished during the Period for which he shall have been elected, and he shall not receive within that Period any other Emolument from the United States, or any of them.

Before he enter on the Execution of his Office, he shall take the following Oath or Affirmation:—"I do solemnly swear (or affirm) that I will faithfully execute the Office of President of the United States, and will to the best of my Ability, preserve, protect and defend the Constitution of the United States."

Section. 2.

The President shall be Commander in Chief of the Army and Navy of the United States, and of the Militia of the several States, when called into the actual Service of the United States; he may require the Opinion, in writing, of the principal Officer in each of the executive Departments, upon any Subject relating to the Duties of their respective Offices, and he shall have Power to grant Reprieves and Pardons for Offences against the United States, except in Cases of Impeachment.

He shall have Power, by and with the Advice and Consent of the Senate, to make Treaties, provided two thirds of the Senators present concur; and he shall nominate, and by and with the Advice and Consent of the Senate, shall appoint Ambassadors, other public Ministers and Consuls, Judges of the supreme Court, and all other Officers of the United States, whose Appointments are not herein otherwise provided for, and which shall be established by Law: but the Congress may by Law vest the Appointment of such inferior Officers, as they think proper, in the President alone, in the Courts of Law, or in the Heads of Departments.

The President shall have Power to fill up all Vacancies that may happen during the Recess of the Senate, by granting Commissions which shall expire at the End of their next Session.

Section. 3.

He shall from time to time give to the Congress Information of the State of the Union, and recommend to their Consideration such Measures as he shall judge necessary and expedient; he may, on extraordinary Occasions, convene both Houses, or either of them, and in Case of Disagreement between them, with Respect to the Time of Adjournment, he may adjourn them to such Time as he shall think proper; he shall receive Ambassadors and other public Ministers; he shall take Care that the Laws be faithfully executed, and shall Commission all the Officers of the United States.

Section. 4.
The President, Vice President and all civil Officers of the United States, shall be removed from Office on Impeachment for, and Conviction of, Treason, Bribery, or other high Crimes and Misdemeanors.

Article. III.

Section. 1.
The judicial Power of the United States, shall be vested in one supreme Court, and in such inferior Courts as the Congress may from time to time ordain and establish. The Judges, both of the supreme and inferior Courts, shall hold their Offices during good Behaviour, and shall, at stated Times, receive for their Services, a Compensation, which shall not be diminished during their Continuance in Office.

Section. 2.
The judicial Power shall extend to all Cases, in Law and Equity, arising under this Constitution, the Laws of the United States, and Treaties made, or which shall be made, under their Authority;—to all Cases affecting Ambassadors, other public Ministers and Consuls;—to all Cases of admiralty and maritime Jurisdiction;—to Controversies to which the United States shall be a Party;—to Controversies between two or more States;— between a State and Citizens of another State,—between Citizens of different States,—between Citizens of the same State claiming Lands under Grants of different States, and between a State, or the Citizens thereof, and foreign States, Citizens or Subjects.

In all Cases affecting Ambassadors, other public Ministers and Consuls, and those in which a State shall be Party, the supreme Court shall have original Jurisdiction. In all the other Cases before mentioned, the supreme Court shall have appellate Jurisdiction, both as to Law and Fact, with such Exceptions, and under such Regulations as the Congress shall make.

The Trial of all Crimes, except in Cases of Impeachment, shall be by Jury; and such Trial shall be held in the State where the said Crimes shall have been committed; but when not committed within any State, the Trial shall be at such Place or Places as the Congress may by Law have directed.

Section. 3.
Treason against the United States, shall consist only in levying War against them, or in adhering to their Enemies, giving them Aid and Comfort. No Person shall be convicted of Treason unless on the Testimony of two Witnesses to the same overt Act, or on Confession in open Court.

The Congress shall have Power to declare the Punishment of Treason, but no Attainder of Treason shall work Corruption of Blood, or Forfeiture except during the Life of the Person attainted.

Article. IV.

Section. 1.
Full Faith and Credit shall be given in each State to the public Acts, Records, and judicial Proceedings of every other State. And the Congress may by general Laws prescribe the Manner in which such Acts, Records and Proceedings shall be proved, and the Effect thereof.

Section. 2.
The Citizens of each State shall be entitled to all Privileges and Immunities of Citizens in the several States.

A Person charged in any State with Treason, Felony, or other Crime, who shall flee from Justice, and be found in another State, shall on

Demand of the executive Authority of the State from which he fled, be delivered up, to be removed to the State having Jurisdiction of the Crime.

No Person held to Service or Labour in one State, under the Laws thereof, escaping into another, shall, in Consequence of any Law or Regulation therein, be discharged from such Service or Labour, but shall be delivered up on Claim of the Party to whom such Service or Labour may be due.

Section. 3.
New States may be admitted by the Congress into this Union; but no new State shall be formed or erected within the Jurisdiction of any other State; nor any State be formed by the Junction of two or more States, or Parts of States, without the Consent of the Legislatures of the States concerned as well as of the Congress.

The Congress shall have Power to dispose of and make all needful Rules and Regulations respecting the Territory or other Property belonging to the United States; and nothing in this Constitution shall be so construed as to Prejudice any Claims of the United States, or of any particular State.

Section. 4.
The United States shall guarantee to every State in this Union a Republican Form of Government, and shall protect each of them against Invasion; and on Application of the Legislature, or of the Executive (when the Legislature cannot be convened) against domestic Violence.

Article. V.

The Congress, whenever two thirds of both Houses shall deem it necessary, shall propose Amendments to this Constitution, or, on the Application of the Legislatures of two-thirds of the several States, shall call a Convention for proposing Amendments, which, in either Case, shall be valid to all Intents and Purposes, as Part of this Constitution, when ratified by the Legislatures of three-fourths of the several States, or by Conventions in three fourths thereof, as the one or the other Mode of Ratification may be proposed by the

Congress; Provided that no Amendment which may be made prior to the Year One thousand eight hundred and eight shall in any Manner affect the first and fourth Clauses in the Ninth Section of the first Article; and that no State, without its Consent, shall be deprived of its equal Suffrage in the Senate.

Article. VI.
All Debts contracted and Engagements entered into, before the Adoption of this Constitution, shall be as valid against the United States under this Constitution, as under the Confederation.

This Constitution, and the Laws of the United States which shall be made in Pursuance thereof; and all Treaties made, or which shall be made, under the Authority of the United States, shall be the supreme Law of the Land; and the Judges in every State shall be bound thereby, any Thing in the Constitution or Laws of any State to the Contrary notwithstanding.

The Senators and Representatives before mentioned, and the Members of the several State Legislatures, and all executive and judicial Officers, both of the United States and of the several States, shall be bound by Oath or Affirmation, to support this Constitution; but no religious Test shall ever be required as a Qualification to any Office or public Trust under the United States.

Article. VII.
The Ratification of the Conventions of nine States, shall be sufficient for the Establishment of this Constitution between the States so ratifying the Same.

The Word, "the," being interlined between the seventh and eighth Lines of the first Page, The Word "Thirty" being partly written on an Erazure in the fifteenth Line of the first Page, The Words "is tried" being interlined between the thirty second and thirty third Lines of the first Page and the Word "the" being interlined between the forty third and forty fourth Lines of the second Page.

Attest William Jackson Secretary

done in Convention by the Unanimous Consent of the States present the Seventeenth Day of September in the Year of our Lord one thousand seven hundred and Eighty-seven and of the Independence of the United States of America the Twelfth In witness whereof We have hereunto subscribed our Names,

G°. Washington
President and deputy from Virginia

Delaware
Geo: Read
Gunning Bedford jun
John Dickinson
Richard Bassett
Jaco: Broom

Maryland
James McHenry
Dan of St Thos. Jenifer
Danl. Carroll

Virginia
John Blair
James Madison Jr.

North Carolina
Wm. Blount
Richd. Dobbs Spaight
Hu Williamson

South Carolina
J. Rutledge
Charles Cotesworth Pinckney
Charles Pinckney
Pierce Butler

Georgia
William Few
Abr Baldwin

New Hampshire
John Langdon
Nicholas Gilman

Massachusetts
Nathaniel Gorham
Rufus King

Connecticut
Wm. Saml. Johnson
Roger Sherman

New York
Alexander Hamilton

New Jersey
Wil: Livingston
David Brearley
Wm. Paterson
Jona: Dayton

Pennsylvania
B Franklin
Thomas Mifflin
Robt. Morris
Geo. Clymer
Thos. FitzSimons
Jared Ingersoll
James Wilson
Gouv Morris

The Bill of Rights Ratified December 15th 1791

ARTICLES in addition to, and Amendment of the Constitution of the United States of America, proposed by Congress and ratified by the Legislatures of the several States, pursuant to the fifth Article of the original Constitution.

Article the first... After the first enumeration required by the first article of the Constitution, there shall be one Representative for every thirty thousand, until the number shall amount to one hundred, after which the proportion shall be so regulated by Congress, that there shall be not less than one hundred Representatives, nor less than one Representative for every forty thousand persons, until the number of Representatives shall amount to two hundred; after which the proportion shall be so regulated by Congress, that there shall not be less than two hundred Representatives, nor more than one Representative for every fifty thousand persons.

Article the second... No law, varying the compensation for the services of the Senators and Representatives, shall take effect, until an election of Representatives shall have intervened.

Article the third... Congress shall make no law respecting an establishment of religion, or prohibiting the free exercise thereof; or abridging the freedom of speech, or of the press; or the right of the people peaceably to assemble, and to petition the Government for a redress of grievances.

Article the fourth... A well regulated Militia, being necessary to the security of a free State, the right of the people to keep and bear Arms, shall not be infringed.

Article the fifth... No Soldier shall, in time of peace be quartered in any house, without the consent of the Owner, nor in time of war, but in a manner to be prescribed by law.

Article the sixth... The right of the people to be secure in their persons, houses, papers, and effects, against unreasonable searches and seizures, shall not be violated, and no Warrants shall issue, but upon probable cause, supported by Oath or affirmation, and particularly describing the place to be searched, and the persons or things to be seized.

Article the seventh... No person shall be held to answer for a capital, or otherwise infamous crime, unless on a presentment or indictment of a Grand Jury, except in cases arising in the land or naval forces, or in the Militia, when in actual service in time of War or public danger; nor shall any person be subject for the same offence to be twice put in jeopardy of life or limb; nor shall be compelled in any criminal case to be a witness against himself, nor be deprived of life, liberty, or property, without due process of law; nor shall private property be taken for public use, without just compensation.

Article the eighth... In all criminal prosecutions, the accused shall enjoy the right to a speedy and public trial, by an impartial jury of the State and district wherein the crime shall have been committed, which district shall have been previously ascertained by law, and to be informed of the nature and cause of the accusation; to be confronted with the witnesses against him; to have compulsory process for obtaining witnesses in his favor, and to have the Assistance of Counsel for his defence.

Article the ninth... In suits at common law, where the value in controversy shall exceed twenty dollars, the right of trial by jury shall be preserved, and no fact tried by a jury, shall be otherwise re-examined in any Court of the United States, than according to the rules of the common law.

Article the tenth... Excessive bail shall not be required, nor excessive fines imposed, nor cruel and unusual punishments inflicted.

Article the eleventh... The enumeration in the Constitution, of certain rights, shall not be construed to deny or disparage others retained by the people.

Article the twelfth... The powers not delegated to the United States by the Constitution, nor prohibited by it to the States, are reserved to the States respectively, or to the people.

ATTEST,

Frederick Augustus Muhlenberg, Speaker of the House of Representatives
John Adams, Vice-President of the United States, and President of the Senate
John Beckley, Clerk of the House of Representatives.
Sam. A Otis Secretary of the Senate

Appendix B

What Chat GBT Has to Say

Just for fun and confirmation let's see what Chat GBT has to say about the harmful effects of deception by those that we hired to lead and those we trusted to sell us products verified as safe by Government endorsing agencies. The titles are what I asked it.

Title: The Case for a Fourth Branch of Government: Combating Deception in the United States

Introduction
In an era marked by misinformation, manipulation, and deceit, the United States finds itself grappling with the challenges posed by deceptive practices. To address this pressing issue and safeguard the integrity of democratic processes, it is essential to consider the establishment of a fourth branch of government dedicated to outlawing deception. This article presents a compelling argument for the creation of such a branch, highlighting the benefits it would bring in countering misinformation, protecting public trust, and promoting transparency.

I. Upholding the Principle of Truth
The foundation of a functional democracy rests on the principle of truth. A fourth branch of government dedicated to outlawing deception would prioritize the dissemination of accurate information and combat the spread of false narratives. By establishing clear legal guidelines and standards, this branch could hold individuals and entities accountable for intentionally spreading misinformation, ensuring that public discourse is grounded in truth.

II. Preserving Democratic Processes

Deception undermines the very fabric of democratic processes. It erodes trust in institutions, distorts public opinion, and hinders informed decision-making. A fourth branch of government would work to preserve the integrity of elections, political campaigns, and public debates by penalizing deliberate attempts to deceive the electorate. Such a branch could enforce stricter regulations on political advertisements, require fact-checking mechanisms, and hold candidates accountable for misleading statements.

III. Strengthening Public Trust

A key element of a well-functioning democracy is the trust between the government and its citizens. By actively combating deception, a fourth branch of government would help restore and strengthen public trust. Through rigorous oversight, investigation, and enforcement of anti-deception laws, this branch would serve as a beacon of transparency, ensuring that the government operates with honesty and integrity.

IV. Promoting Accountability and Responsibility

A dedicated branch focused on outlawing deception would not only hold individuals accountable but also foster a culture of responsibility. It would discourage politicians, media outlets, and individuals from spreading false information by imposing penalties, including fines, public reprimands, and, in extreme cases, criminal charges. By creating a clear legal framework to address deceptive practices, this branch would deter potential deceivers and incentivize responsible behavior.

V. Safeguarding National Security

Deception poses a significant threat to national security, making it imperative to address this issue comprehensively. A fourth branch of government could collaborate with intelligence agencies and cybersecurity experts to counter disinformation campaigns and foreign interference. By actively monitoring and exposing deceptive tactics employed by foreign entities, this branch would safeguard the nation's security interests and preserve the sovereignty of democratic processes.

Conclusion
In an age dominated by misinformation and manipulation, the establishment of a fourth branch of government dedicated to outlawing deception is a necessary and timely step for the United States. By upholding the principles of truth, preserving democratic processes, strengthening public trust, promoting accountability and responsibility, and safeguarding national security, this branch would contribute to a healthier and more transparent democracy. It is through such dedicated efforts that the United States can fortify its democratic institutions and protect the integrity of public discourse, ensuring that the nation moves forward with honesty and fairness.

Then I asked it another question as I drilled down on the issue.

Title: The Devastating Effects of Deception from Trusted Authority Figures

Introduction
Trust is a fundamental element of human interaction, and when that trust is shattered through deception, the consequences can be profound. Particularly devastating is the impact of deception when it comes from authority figures we place our faith in. Whether it's a parent, teacher, religious leader, or government official, the betrayal of trust from someone we believe to have our best interests at heart can have far-reaching effects on an individual's emotional, psychological, and social well-being. This article explores the profound consequences of deception from trusted authority figures, shedding light on the deep wounds it can inflict.

I. Betrayal and Erosion of Trust
When an authority figure deceives us, the very foundation of trust crumbles. Trust is the glue that holds relationships together, and when it is broken, it can be extremely difficult to repair. Deception from a trusted authority figure leaves a lasting impact, leading to feelings of betrayal, disillusionment, and skepticism toward others. The victim may question their own judgment and become wary of

placing trust in anyone else, making it challenging to form healthy relationships in the future.

II. Emotional and Psychological Trauma
Deception from a trusted authority figure can cause severe emotional and psychological trauma. The shock and disbelief that follow the revelation of the deception can lead to intense feelings of anger, hurt, and confusion. The person may experience a deep sense of loss, as the authority figure they once admired is now seen in a completely different light. This emotional turmoil can result in symptoms of depression, anxiety, post-traumatic stress disorder (PTSD), and even trust-related disorders.

III. Self-Identity and Self-Esteem
Deception from an authority figure can deeply affect a person's sense of self. When someone we trust deceives us, it can shatter our self-perception and self-worth. The victim may question their own judgment, instincts, and ability to discern truth from falsehood. They may also experience a loss of confidence and struggle with feelings of inadequacy and self-doubt. The impact on self-identity can be long-lasting, making it difficult for individuals to rebuild their sense of self and regain their self-esteem.

IV. Impact on Decision-Making and Autonomy
Deception from a trusted authority figure can erode a person's ability to make decisions and assert their autonomy. When someone we trust deceives us, it can lead to a loss of confidence in our own decision-making abilities. Victims may become hesitant to trust their instincts and make choices, fearing they will be deceived once again. This can result in a cycle of indecision, self-doubt, and a diminished sense of control over one's life.

V. Social and Interpersonal Challenges
Deception from a trusted authority figure can have far-reaching effects on a person's social interactions and relationships. The victim may develop difficulties in trusting others, leading to challenges in forming close connections and friendships. They may become overly cautious and guarded, fearing that others may also deceive or betray

them. These challenges can result in social isolation, strained relationships, and difficulties in building healthy support networks.

Conclusion

Deception from a trusted authority figure is a deeply traumatic experience that leaves lasting scars on an individual's emotional, psychological, and social well-being. The betrayal of trust undermines the very foundations of human relationships and can have devastating effects on a person's self-perception, decision-making, and ability to form healthy connections. Recognizing the profound impact of deception is essential, as it allows for the understanding and support necessary for individuals to heal and rebuild their lives. It is crucial for society to foster a culture of transparency, integrity, and honesty to be strong.

Ok, you've heard what I have to say, and an AI, what say you about this? Do you want to end harmful deception and put our country back to its mission statement goals? I will be adding your comments gathered from the Creating Paradise YoutTube, Rumble and X channels. I look forward to working with you to build the better future I know the 4th Branch of US Government can bring. I will love to add your comments to this book, I have room for about 20 using up to 400 characters, but really, no limits but would like to include everyone one of you who would like to contribute. I know, get a blog site, I will in due time.

Appendix C

Fallacious and Correct Methods of Conducting an Argument in the Pursuit of Truth.

To get to the truth of an issue one must first discard any fallacious way of thinking that could become a communication. These are judgment filters we can or cannot use to judge incoming information which is the process of setting up bias filters in your problem-solving skill set. Let's take a look at what these biases or fallacies are so we can be aware of them and thereby enter the argument at hand with the clearest mindset possible.

They are named in the Greek root word title followed by with the common English descriptions.

Argumentum Ad Verecundiam - the appeal of authority, letting an authority decide what is true. It is equally a fallacy to assume that just because someone is not a recognized authority on a subject that they are wrong.

Argumentum Ad Hominem Attack the person, not the person's talking points. There are 4 types of this sort of attack.

a. Abusive Ad Hominem - Totally disrespecting the person to the point that there is therefore no way his points are true at all.

b. Circumstantial Ad Hominem - a person's circumstances motivate his arguments to his points must be false. The claim is that the person is making his points of argument purely out is self-interest.

c. Guilt by Association - Discrediting an argument, someone's claim to truth, because someone else you do not like agrees with them does not prove their position is false.

d. Ad Hominem Tu Quoque – The bias of claiming someone is false because that person's comments are inconsistent with their previous thoughts or actions. For example, When a person claims A. but does B. This does not disprove A.

Argumentum Ad Baculum – Or Appeal to fair, causing fear in people so they decide with you which does not prove a claim of truth.

Argumentum Ad Populum – The claim that if everyone does it, it must be true. Also known as the bandwagon fallacy. Or appeal to common belief. This is where peer pressure invades to solution process and can hijack it into total suppression.

Argumentum Ad Nauseam – Appeal to repetition. This is stating something is true because it is stated and claimed to be true often in the hopes it will be accepted as true.

Argumentum Ad Antiquitatem - Appeal to common practice. The claim that because everybody does it that it must be true, that is not proof of the claim being true.

The Strawman Fallacy - When one person simply ignores the other person's claim or changes the claim in a way that no longer connects with the original claim or statement completely disregarding the person's original position.

The Non-Sequitur Fallacy – A conclusion or reply that does not follow logically from the previous statements.

Petito Principii - Begging the question. Responding to a question with an answer that does not answer the question, a diverting technique. Also known as circular reasoning, never getting to the heart of the matter, the truth.

Argumnetum Ad Passiones – Appeal to emotions. This is where someone appeals to someone's emotions to get them to accept a claim without actually proving the claim. This method replaces emotions with evidence, which could be the most intrusive fallacy of all.

The Red Herring – Also known as the smoke screen or wild goose chase. This is another means to divert attention from the original issue, often used by politicians. The strategy is to lead the argument away from the issue in order to win the argument.

Argumentum Ad Ridiculum – Also known as appeal to ridicule. This fallacy uses sarcasm, ridicule or humor to divert attention away from the issue in order to make the other person look foolish in an attempt to lose the issue in the laugh. It works by presenting the argument in such a way as to make the other person look ridiculous. Usually by misinterpreting the argument which can be by the use of exaggerations.

The Middle Ground Fallacy – This fallacy assumes that the middle position between the two extremes must be the correct one. This is an escapist attitude because it does not seek the truth, it is another diversion. And please keep in mind, this is not at all what the trinity balance of opposites in the book teaches because the time and space domains CREATE the unifying force, both are needed and to solve for truth in a subject is therefore a task of finding the quality and quality of each of the time and space elements. Write me if you have any trouble with this one.

The Relativist Fallacy – This is where one person rejects a claim saying that it might be true for others but not for them. This is a sign of a closed mind, so just walk away slowly and let them be unless you care enough to help them. They are not using reason.

The following are not fallacies in finding the truth, they are the methods that work, but they are not the best to use.

Ockham's Razor – This is where someone has to choose between two explanations for an uncertain situation. One uses logic and reason to choose the most logical explanation between the ones being considered. This will let you draw a conclusion but it still may not be the truth.

Rigid Skepticism – Being skeptical is a good thing but some are so much so that they reject everything and anything that does not fit in with their conclusions. This is an extremely closed-mind position one can be in, but again, being skeptical is a good thing. You do not want to simply accept what someone is saying as truth, you still want your open mind to prove or disprove what you are hearing in order to understand what something is.

Apophasis – Affirmation through negation, or the apophasis injury. Removing something from the argument is something that it is not. Or seeking first to find what something is not.

These three are the best ways to find the truth that I know

Nash Equilibrium – This method aims at revealing the true meaning behind any discussion ensuring that both parties learn something from such an effort. This is a good aim because it ensures growth and learning, the true purpose of talking with one another about anything. It can be said to be derived from the root meaning of the word, conversation, whereas Con = together and versation = change, together we change is what conversation means, so keep that in mind when bringing up subjects to another, you too are in the cross hairs to change to, not just the listener.

Trinity Balance Formula – This method works by finding the most absolute truth of the three core domain descriptions of the subject. These are categorized by the absolute time, space, and frequency domains listed in chapter two herein. This method is good for finding the three basic balance of components of a whole thing, which is a good practice to know and use so you can be more accurate and functional in your use of terms and applications thereof. The next step after this is to use this in your usage of the scientific method to get to workable applications. (This method is from my Trinity Balance book).

The Scientific Method - This is what The Britannica Encyclopedia says about how to use this method: "A researcher develops a hypothesis motivated by his or her observations, tests it through various means, and then modifies the hypothesis on the basis of the outcome of the tests and experiments. The modified hypothesis is then retested, further modified, and tested again until it becomes consistent with observed phenomena and testing outcomes. In this way, hypotheses serve as tools by which scientists gather data. From that data and the many scientific investigations undertaken to explore hypotheses, scientists can develop broad general explanations or scientific theories."

These are the methods that do and don't work in the truth discovery process. I trust you will use those that inspire integrity and honesty within you as you seek your truth, the truth in a situation, thing, or event. Using the purest and tested method we have to question what is claimed to be true is at the heart of the 4th Branch of Governments' mission process of discovery. And again, know that any finding will always be up for a challenge including how it comes to a conclusion.

References

1. Barry Lyons The Cancer Cure that worked: fifty Years of Suppression 1987

2. Edward T. Haslam (Author), Jim Marrs (Foreword)

   Dr. Mary's Monkey: How the Unsolved Murder of a Doctor, a Secret Laboratory in New Orleans and Cancer-Causing Monkey Viruses Are Linked to Lee Harvey ... Assassination and Emerging Global Epidemics 1965

I know, I need to show a lot more, I will get to it and yeah, accepting all suggestions and help in any way including donations you can go to this "go fund me" page: https://www.gofundme.com/f/adding-two-new-amendments-to-the-us-constitution as this will not be cheap due to court costs, but let's see if that too can be not expensive, like the whole of this solution is to get into your hands. Any and all funds out side of expenses to fund base level of this project will go to said court case and ballot inclusion in the earliest possible general election that we can include out amendments for a vote.

And to network with me and others on how to grow this proposal into reality visit my utube, rumble and or X channel to talk about it. Together we can end the infection of selfish greed in our servant, the US Government.

Made in the USA
Monee, IL
08 November 2026

67380776R00057